Recess Time

Patterns

Lisa Greathouse

Consultants

Chandra C. Prough, M.S.Ed.
National Board Certified
Newport-Mesa
  Unified School District

Jodene Smith, M.A.
ABC Unified School District

Publishing Credits

Dona Herweck Rice, *Editor-in-Chief*
Lee Aucoin, *Creative Director*
Chris McIntyre, M.A.Ed., *Editorial Director*
James Anderson, M.S.Ed., *Editor*
Aubrie Nielsen, M.S.Ed., *Associate Education Editor*
Neri Garcia, *Senior Designer*
Stephanie Reid, *Photo Editor*
Rachelle Cracchiolo, M.S.Ed., *Publisher*

Teacher Created Materials

5301 Oceanus Drive
Huntington Beach, CA 92649-1030
http://www.tcmpub.com
ISBN 978-1-4333-3436-8
© 2012 Teacher Created Materials, Inc.
BP 5028

Table of Contents

You play at recess.

You can look for patterns, too!

Slides are different sizes.

Some are tall.

Some are short.

Slides can make a pattern.

A pattern **repeats**.

This is an AB pattern.

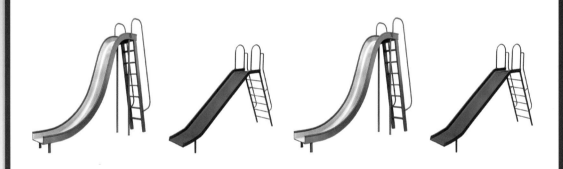

A   B   A   B

Rings are shapes.
Some are circles.
Some are triangles.

Rings can make a pattern.

This is an AB pattern.

A B A B

Toys are in the sandbox.

Some are big.

Some are little.

Toys can make a pattern.

This is an ABB pattern.

A   **B**   **B**

A   **B**   **B**

Yo-yos can move.
They go up.
They go down.

Yo-yos can make a pattern.

This is an AB pattern.

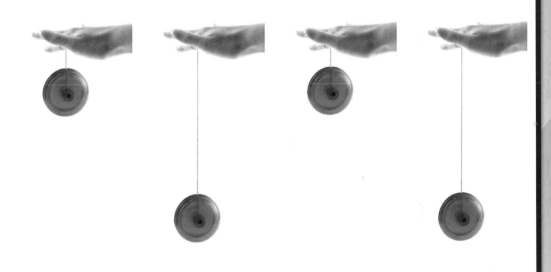

A   B   A   B

Parachutes can be many colors.

This one is blue, red, and green.

Parachutes can make a pattern.

This is an ABC pattern.

A B C A B C

Hopscotch is fun!
You can hop and jump.

Hopscotch can make a pattern.

This is an AAB pattern.

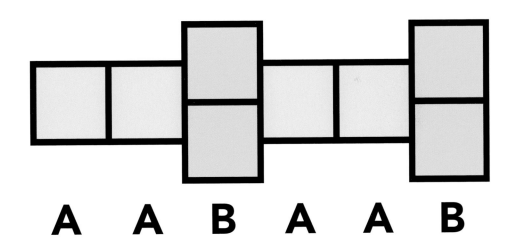

A A B A A B

A clapping game is fun, too. You can clap and snap.

A clapping game can make a pattern.

This is an AAB pattern.

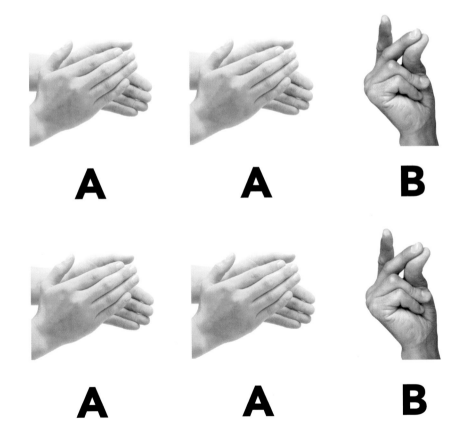

A   A   B

A   A   B

Balls are on the grass.

They are yellow and blue.

Balls can make a pattern.

This is an ABB pattern.

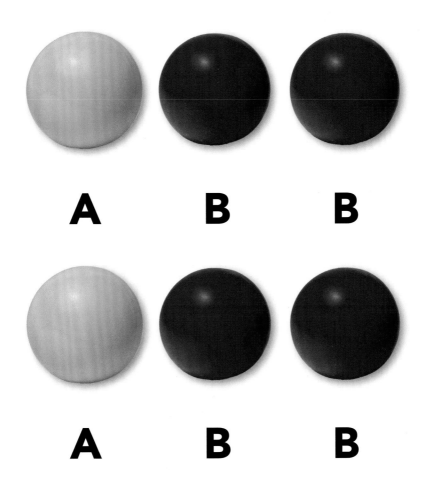

A   B   B

A   B   B

Swings make you fly high!

They go forward and back.

Swings can make a pattern.

This is an AB pattern.

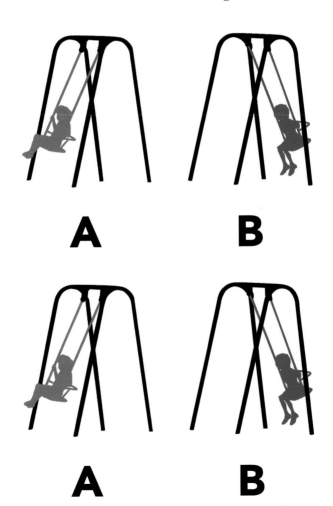

A   **B**

A   **B**

Balls are used in many games.
Look at the pattern.

1. Point to the kind of ball that comes next.

2. What kind of pattern is shown?

Look at the pattern.

1. Who comes next?

2. What kind of pattern is shown?

What patterns can you make with blocks?

Materials

✓ pattern blocks

1 Make a shape pattern with the blocks.

2 Name your pattern with letters.

3 Try to make a color pattern.

4 Can you make another pattern?

Glossary

patterns—designs that repeat

repeats—happens more than one time

Patterns

A B

A A B

A B B

A B C

You Try It!

Pages 24–25:

1.

2. ABC

Pages 26–27:

1.

2. AAB

Solve the Problem

Answers will vary.